WHALES, WHALING AND WHALECRAFT

By Paul Giambarba

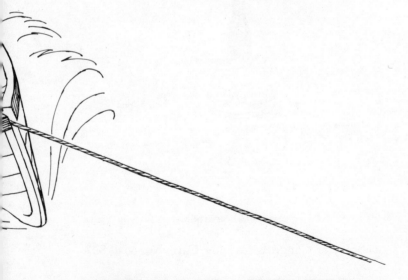

SCRIMSHAW PUBLISHING

The Scrimshaw Press of Centerville, Massachusetts

1967

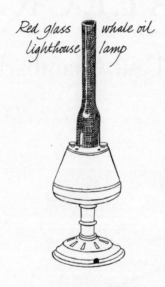

Red glass whale oil lighthouse lamp

FIRST PRINTING 1967

Library of Congress Catalog Card No. 66-19827

Printed in the United States of America

CONTENTS

The Whaler's World

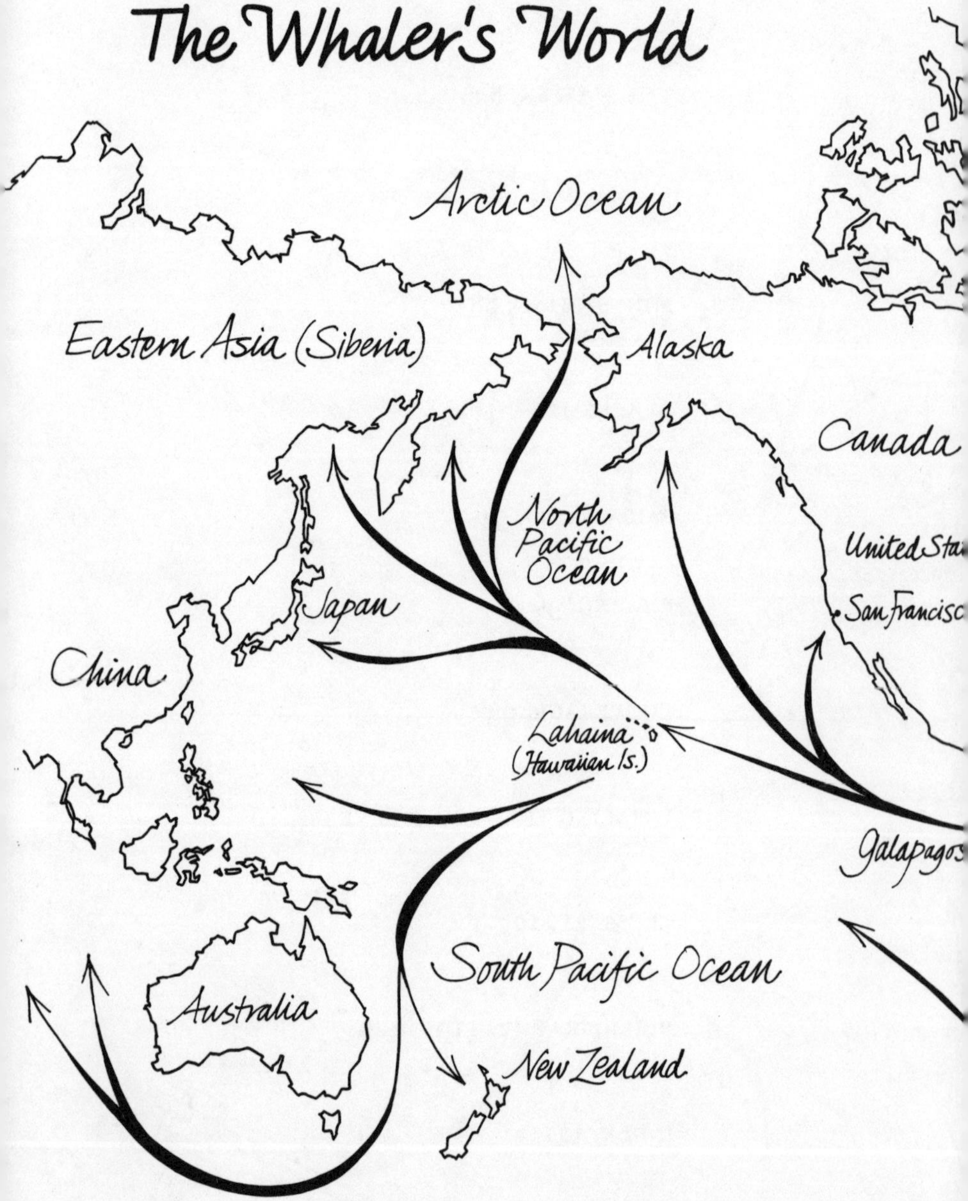

Arctic Ocean

Eastern Asia (Siberia)

Alaska

Canada

United Stat

North
Pacific
Ocean

San Francisc

Japan

China

Lahaina
(Hawaiian Is.)

Galapagos

South Pacific Ocean

Australia

New Zealand

Greenland

Greenland Sea

Barents Sea

Iceland

North
Atlantic Ocean

Asia

America

New Bedford

Nantucket

Azores Is.

Bay of
Biscay

Europe

Canary Is.

India

Cape Verde Is.

Africa

Indian Ocean

Paita

South America

Valparaiso

Madagascar I.

Cape of Good Hope

South
Atlantic Ocean

Cape Horn

WHALES, WHALING AND WHALECRAFT

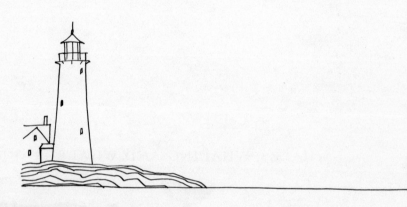

The Need for Whale Oil

The need for oil goes back as far as man's need for light. For thousands of years oil lit the lamps of the world and whale oil was superior to all other kinds.

Whales were hunted because of the great amounts of oil they yielded. The capture, killing and processing of a full grown whale provided an enormous quantity of oil. A single bowhead whale, a type of right whale (see page 22) found in the Arctic yielded over 250 barrels or 7,875 gallons of oil! In the days before oil wells, this was the equivalent of a lucky strike or "gusher."

For years oil from the sperm whale was burned in the lamps of lighthouses, and was also the best lubricant for machinery that was known at the time. In many respects it still is because it stays fluid and doesn't congeal at low temperatures.

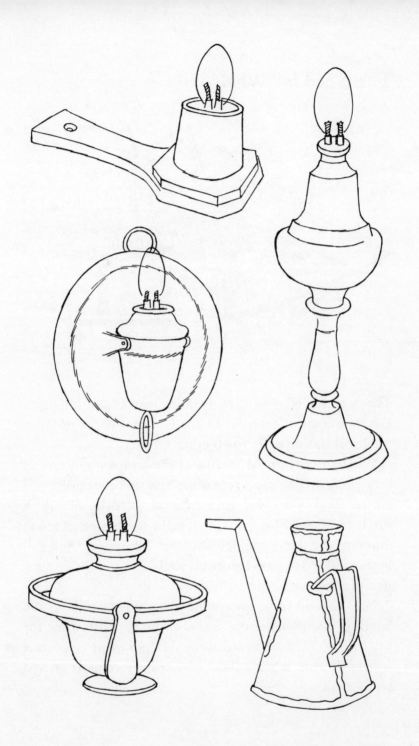

Whale Oil Lamps

Whale oil lamps of all kinds, from the hand-held ship-board lamp that was used between decks, to the huge lamps that illuminated lighthouses, generally had two wicks instead of one. It was thought that the heat from one burning wick would help the other to draw more oil from the storage tank of the lamp. The twisted cotton wick had to be trimmed as it burned and the glass lenses of the lamps kept spotless by constant cleaning and polishing.

On the facing page we see at the top a shipboard lamp with a wood handle that could be carried by hand or fitted on a wooden pin when used as an overhead lamp.

Below it, left, are two versions of whale oil lamps on gimbals. A gimbal is a device that keeps a fixture level no matter how much a vessel might pitch and roll.

The large lamp, right, is made of pewter and was used as a living room, or "parlor" lamp.

The curious container at the right bottom is a tin whale oil can used to fill the tanks of the lamps.

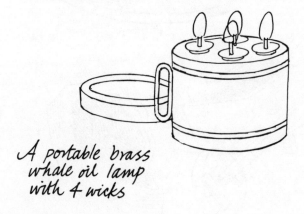

A portable brass whale oil lamp with 4 wicks

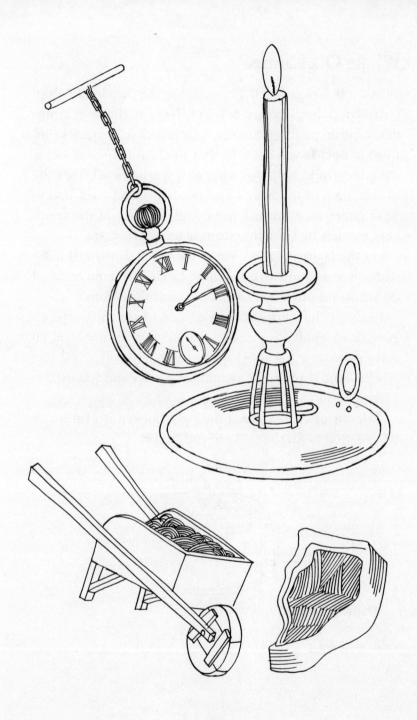

Other Uses

Whale oil was also used to lubricate watches. Certain types of oil such as that from the head or "melon" of the pilot whale or blackfish (page 30) made excellent lubricants that could withstand great changes in temperature.

The head of the sperm whale contains a great "case" or reservoir of spermaceti, a thick, whitish oil that becomes waxy when exposed to air. This was shipped home and processed in huge presses to make sperm oil candles which were smokeless.

Sperm oil was also prized as an ointment with great healing power, according to the folklore of the time.

Nowadays the bones of whales are ground up to make fertilizers for crops.

Whale meat has been eaten for thousands of years by Eskimos, Scandinavians, and Japanese.

Ambergris (page 35), a tarry substance found in the stomachs of sperm whales, was widely used in the manufacture of perfumes.

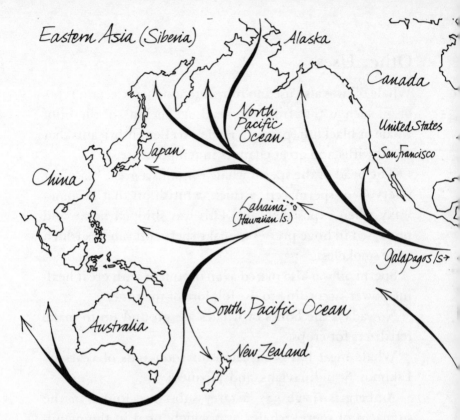

Eastern Asia (Siberia) Alaska

Canada

North Pacific Ocean

United States
San Francisco

China

Japan

Lahaina
(Hawaiian Is.)

Galapagos Is.→

South Pacific Ocean

Australia

New Zealand

The Whaler's World

Yankee whalers were some of the first to round Cape Horn
and enter the South Pacific Ocean. It was the voyages of
these whalers that hastened the settlement of Australia and
New Zealand. Whale hunters were the first Americans to
enter Japanese waters and were almost the only explorers
of the Arctic Ocean.

The ports they called at were remote and sometimes for-
bidding. This helped to discourage the crew from "jumping ship" or deserting. In port they took on water, fruit
and "shipped" or replenished the crew: Cape Verdeans,
Azoreans, Fiji Islanders, Samoans, Kanakas from the Sand-
wich Isles (Hawaii).

[18]

Honolulu and Lahaina in the Hawaiian island of Maui were ports of call for refitting, shipping oil, and liberty for the crews.

At the Galapagos Islands turtles were caught and fresh water taken on.

Russell Bay of Islands, New Zealand, was a supply, shipping and liberty port.

The Azores Islands were a supply and recruitment port for outbound vessels.

San Francisco was a refitting, shipping, and liberty port. Many men deserted here when the Gold Rush fever was high (1849-1850).

Paita, Peru, and Valparaiso, Chile, were supply and liberty ports.

Sperm Whale

Physeter catadon is the scientific name for the largest whale with teeth. The males grow up to 60 feet in length and have been known to yield over 160 barrels of oil. (A barrel of oil is 31½ U. S. gallons.) Cow (female) sperm whales are smaller. Their color is dark bluish gray with lighter undersides. They are distinguished by their long narrow lower jaw with its rows of 20 to 30 teeth on each side.

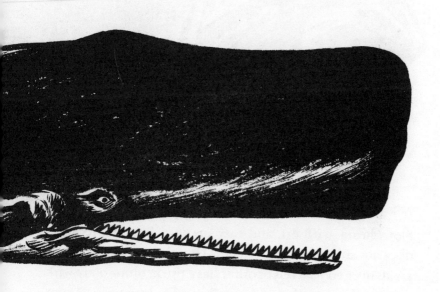

The sperm whale or cachalot fights hard when attacked. In several cases it has rammed and sunk large vessels: Ship *Essex*, Nantucket, 1819, Ship *Ann Alexander*, New Bedford, 1850, Bark *Kathleen*, 1902.

A white sperm whale is the subject of Herman Melville's book, *Moby Dick*. The sperm whale has one spout hole instead of two, as in the right whale—and is generally found in warm waters.

Right Whale

It was called "right" because it was just right to capture. Slow, heavy with oil, and easy prey for hunters, its body does not sink when it is killed. About 50 feet in length it yields over 200 barrels of oil. It has a thick, blunt body with no dorsal fin or throat furrows, and a bumpy irregular snout or muzzle.

Right whales are black in color, and have baleen instead of teeth. Hairy slats of baleen, or whalebone, are arranged in the whale's upper jaw like vertical venetian blinds and act as a strainer in the whale's mouth.

There are three kinds of right whales: the bowhead, or Greenland Right Whale (*Balaena mysticetus*), the Biscayan Right Whale (*Eubalaena glacialis*) and the Pigmy Right Whale (*Caperea marginata*). The bowhead has a huge head with a curved bowlike mouth. It is found in Arctic waters. The Biscayan right whale's name comes from the Bay of Biscay, between France and Spain—where it was hunted by Basque whalers over 700 years ago. This was the "right" whale first taken by American whalers off the New England shore. It ranges all over the Atlantic and Pacific. The Pigmy right whale is rare, and lives in the Antarctic Ocean off the shores of Australia, New Zealand, and South America.

Fin Back Whale

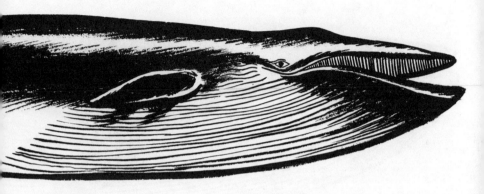

Balaenoptera physalus is the fastest whale of all—and one of the largest. From 50 to 80 feet in length, the fin back is recognizable by its long slender body and graceful lines, prominent dorsal fin, and furrowed throat.

It is dark gray with white undersides. A fin back's spout will reach 15 to 20 feet in the air. These whales are found in all the large oceans and they usually assemble in schools.

Because of its speed and small proportion of oil, the fin back was not hunted as much as other whales were.

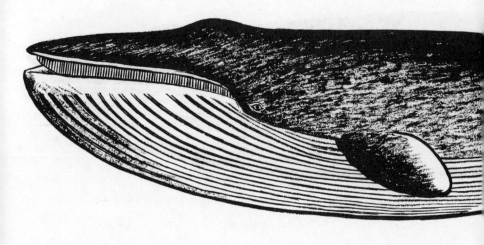

Blue Whale

Balaenoptera musculus is the largest of all whales, indeed of all living creatures. It reaches a length of over 80 or 90 feet. Females are larger and some rare giants over 100 feet long have been caught. These monsters weigh well over 100 tons and yield over 150 barrels of oil (or 4,725 gallons).

Slate blue in color with paler grayish patches, blue whales sometimes have yellowish undersides. From this yellow coloring they earned the name "sulphurbottom."

Blue whales are in danger of becoming extinct from being over-hunted. Those existing live in Arctic or Antarctic waters near the edge of pack ice. They feed on tiny marine life.

Hump Back Whale

Megaptera novaeangliae is distinguished by its smaller size (less than 50 feet), long grotesque flippers which are often encrusted with barnacles, and lumps and knobs on its head. It is black with white undersides.

A playful clown, it can perform acrobatics by leaping clear of the water and belly-flopping with a mighty splash. It can also stand on its nose at times and beat the water into foam with its flukes. Old whalemen called this "lob-tailing." (Sperm whales also lob-tailed.)

The hump back whale is found in all the oceans of the world, following what appears to be a sensible pattern of migration. They winter in the tropics and summer in colder water.

Hump back whales are almost impossible to capture at sea because their bodies sink when dead. Whalers used to capture them in shallow coastal waters where their bodies could be raised.

Other Whales

KILLER WHALE, *Grampus orca,* is easily recognized by its large dorsal fin and bold black and white markings. It has a dozen or so large strong interlocking teeth that can tear apart even the largest whale. Hunting in packs, killer whales will also prey on seals, penguins, and porpoises. The males are up to 30 feet in length. Killer whales are found all over the world.

BOTTLE NOSE DOLPHIN, *Tursiops truncatus,* is common all along the United States Atlantic and Gulf coasts. Up to 12 feet in length, it is named for its curious-shaped nose. It is dark-purplish-grey and white in color. Oil from its head and jaw was used as a watch lubricant.

BLACKFISH, *Globicephala,* gets its name from its dark color and its scientific name from its globular head. Inside the head is a "melon" or reservoir containing around two gallons of valuable oil. Each blackfish yields about 40 gallons of oil from its blubber. The average length is around 15 feet. Many adults reach lengths up to 20 feet.

The blackfish is also known as a pilot whale because of its custom of following a pilot, or guide—even if it means becoming stranded on the beach, which sometimes happens.

A Whale's Life

As all mammals, a whale is a warm-blooded creature. The thick coating of blubber serves as insulation against the cold and pressure of the deep ocean. This is where the whale lives and finds his food. He eats a great quantity and stores his food as fat, or blubber. This is the major source of whale oil. It is tried out (cooked) from the blubber.

The whale is oily and can cry greasy tears. These protect his eyes from being irritated by salt water. His lungs also contain an oily foam which helps to make his breathing, or spouting, visible even in warm weather. The spout is condensed moisture from his breath, such as we see in front of our faces on a cold day.

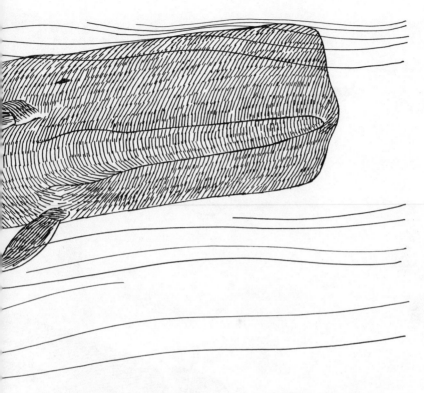

Whales are born in warm waters and back out into a watery world tailfirst, as do dolphins. The calf whale is pushed to the surface by its mother so that it can breathe. The cow whale feeds the calf over 2 gallons of milk a day. It nurses only a few seconds at a time, about fifty times each day.

A whale's blowhole, or nostril, is connected directly with its windpipe and is located on the top of its head. This means water cannot accidentally enter a whale's lungs and cause drowning if its mouth is full of water. The spouting of the whale takes place while breathing. The warm, moist breath is forced from the oily lungs and looks like a small geyser.

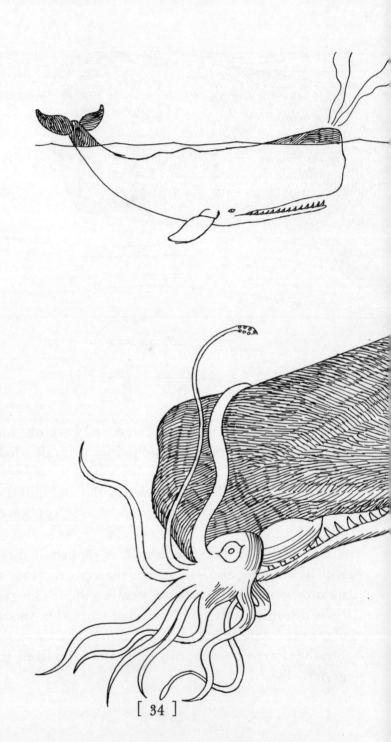

Unlike fish, a whale must rise to the water's surface to breathe, every 10 to 40 minutes, and remains there breathing for about the same length of time before submerging again. Sperm whales can stay under water for over an hour.

The food of whales varies. A sperm whale feeds mainly on the giant squid, devouring a ton of squid (10 legs) and octopus (8 legs) each day. In his search for this food, the sperm whale led his Yankee hunters to remote and uncharted seas.

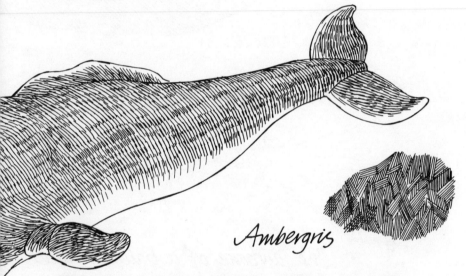

Ambergris

The sperm whale dives 3,000 feet and more, where there is no light from the sun. Some scientists believe it may find its food by sound. Others think the squid may be attracted to the sperm whale's white teeth.

It is often unable to digest the hard parrotlike beak of the squid, which it swallows whole, and these hard pieces form the sticky substance in the stomach that is called ambergris. When the whale is cut up, the ambergris is removed, washed, and sold to perfume manufacturers. It brings a good price—$10 an ounce.

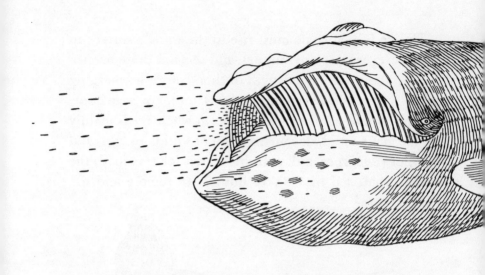

The lower jaw of a Sperm whale

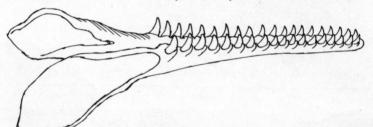

The jawbone of a baleen whale

Baleen, or whalebone, became the chief product of the whaling industry when whale oil was no longer in demand.

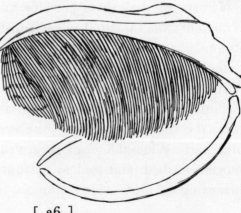

[36]

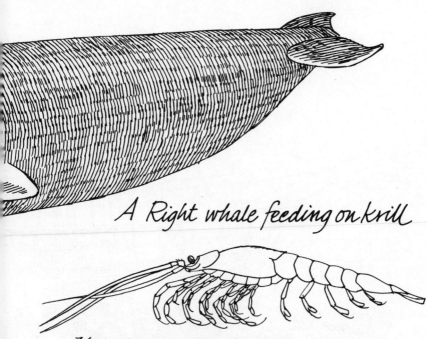

A Right whale feeding on krill

Krill (Euphausia superba) slightly less than life size.

Baleen whales, such as the right whale, and finback, humpback, etc., have very different eating habits. Baleen or whalebone, arranged sideways in their mouths makes a very good strainer or filter. Great gulps of water, "scoops" as the old whalemen called them, are taken into the whale's large mouth. Its huge tongue pushes forward to force the water through the baleen on either side of the mouth.

What remains trapped is the "krill" or "brit," shrimp-like crustaceans and tiny marine animals that cluster on the surface of the ocean. These are then licked down into the gullet.

The coarse, bushy whalebone was saved by whalemen to be used as "horsehair stuffing" in the upholstery of parlor furniture years ago. Strips of heavier baleen were used to provide stays for bodices and bustles, ladies' garments of earlier days.

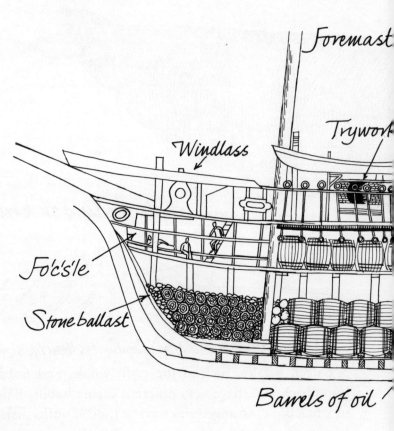

Foremast

Windlass

Trywork

Fo'c'sle

Stone ballast

Barrels of oil

The Whaleship

Broad in the beam, slow and ungainly, the whaleship was scorned by most blue-water sailors.

"Better dead than shipped aboard a blubber-hunter for a four-year cruise," they said, and "whaleships are built by the mile and cut off in lengths as you want 'em."

The last remark refers to the squared-off bow and stern. But whaleships were remarkably well made, many remaining in service over 50 years.

The *Charles W. Morgan,* which can be visited today at Old Mystic Seaport, Connecticut, was built in 1841 and made 37 voyages in its 80 years at sea.

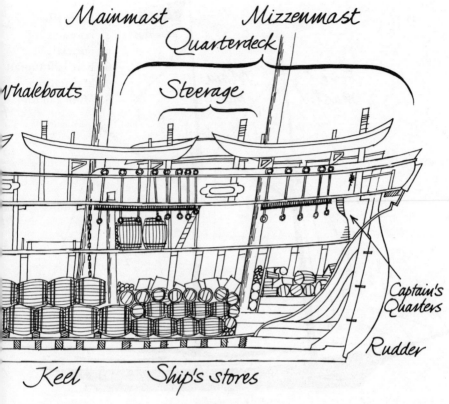

Mainmast   Mizzenmast

Quarterdeck

Whaleboats   Steerage

Captain's Quarters

Rudder

Keel   Ship's stores

Since speed was not essential, as in the case of packets and clipper ships, the whaleships were built for service. They carried a great quantity of gear and special equipment in the brick tryworks, heavy iron try-pots, cooling tanks, whaleboats and the gear for these boats, spare boats and parts, and supplies for the voyage of three years and more. And there had to be room for all those casks of oil!

The officers' quarters were aft, in the stern. The crew, ordinary seamen, were packed up forward, in the low, triangular forecastle—called the fo'c's'le.

In the steerage, aft of amidships, were the quarters of the ship's specialists: harpooners, coopers, carpenter, blacksmith, and cook.

Rigs

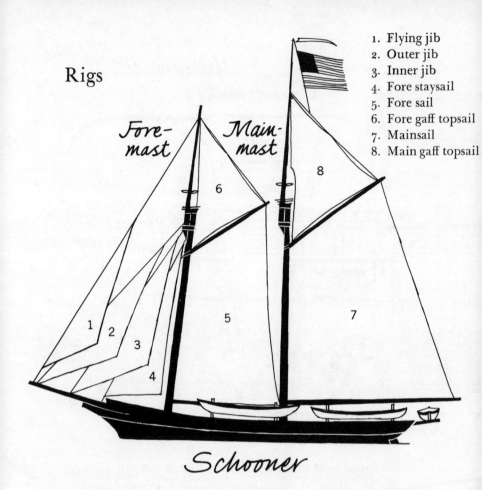

1. Flying jib
2. Outer jib
3. Inner jib
4. Fore staysail
5. Fore sail
6. Fore gaff topsail
7. Mainsail
8. Main gaff topsail

Fore-mast

Main-mast

Schooner

The rigging of whaleships was little different from that of other vessels except for the masthead hoops high in the rigging. In these figure-8-shaped bands the lookouts scoured the sea for the spouts of the whales.

Schooner is usually a two-masted vessel carrying her canvas in a fore-and-aft-rig, though there were many with 3 masts, some with 4, a few with more. Most of the American coasting trade, or the transportation of goods and passengers along the coast, was carried on in schooners. They were remarkably easy to handle, requiring only a small crew to do the work.

Brig

Main-mast

Fore-mast

1. Flying jib
2. Outer jib
3. Inner jib
4. Foresail
5. Fore topsail
6. Fore topgallant sail
7. Fore royal
8. Main topgallant staysail
9. Main topmast staysail
10. Main staysail
11. Mainsail
12. Main gaff topsail

Brig is a two-masted vessel with square sails, except for the fore-and-aft gaff-rigged spanker on the mainmast. The square sail predates the fore-and-aft sail by thousands of years and is much more dependable on the high seas running before the wind in stormy weather.

Most of the sailing done on the open ocean was done in square-rigged vessels.

[41]

Bark is generally a three-masted vessel with square-rigged foremast and mainmast, and a schooner-rigged mizzenmast. Because of its easier handling, this was the most popular type of vessel used in whaling after 1850.

Details of her masts and sails are:

1. Flying jib
2. Outer jib
3. Inner jib
4. Fore staysail
5. Foresail or fore course
6. Fore topsail
7. Fore topgallant sail
8. Fore royal
9. Main royal staysail
10. Main topmast staysail
11. Main staysail
12. Mainsail or main course
13. Main topsail
14. Main topgallant sail
15. Main royal
16. Mizzen topmast staysail
17. Mizzen staysail
18. Spanker or driver
19. Gaff topsail

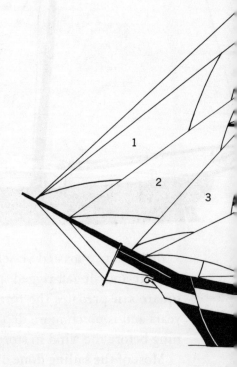

Bark

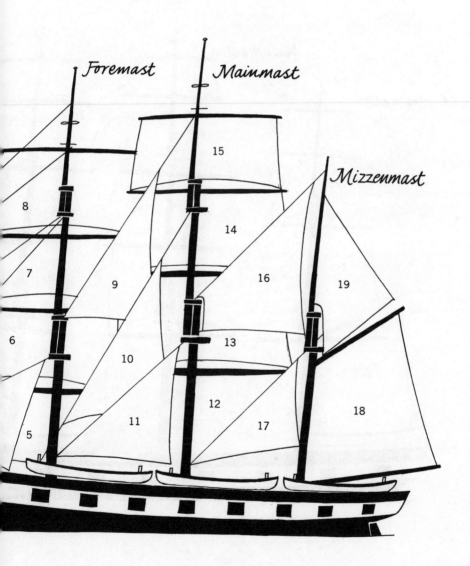

Foremast   Mainmast   Mizzenmast

Ship

Ship is a three-masted square-rigged vessel. Unlike the bark, the ship has square sails on the mizzenmast. The details of the masts and sails are:

1. Flying jib
2. Outer jib
3. Inner jib
4. Fore staysail
5. Foresail or fore course
6. Fore lower topsail
7. Fore upper topsail
8. Fore topgallant sail
9. Fore royal
10. Main royal staysail
11. Main topgallant staysail
12. Main topmast staysail
13. Mainsail or main course
14. Main lower topsail
15. Main upper topsail
16. Main topgallant sail
17. Main royal
18. Mizzen topgallant staysail
19. Mizzen topmast staysail
20. Spanker or driver
21. Mizzen topsail
22. Mizzen topgallant sail
23. Mizzen royal

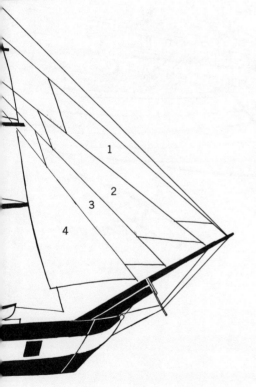

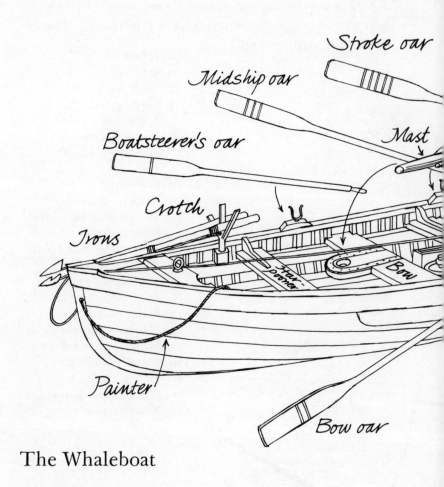

Stroke oar

Midship oar

Boatsteerer's oar

Mast

Crotch

Irons

Bow

Painter

Bow oar

The Whaleboat

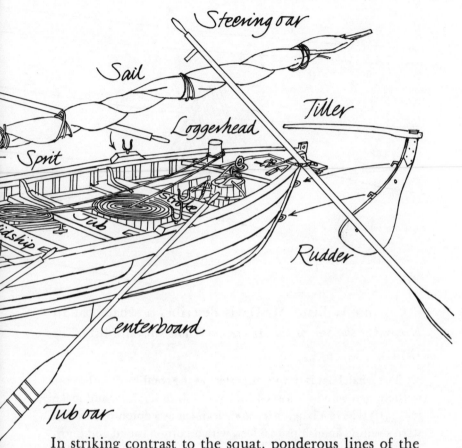

Steering oar

Sail

Tiller

Loggerhead

Sprit

Rudder

Stroke

Tub

Midship

Centerboard

Tub oar

In striking contrast to the squat, ponderous lines of the whaleship, the whaleboats it carried were delicate, beautiful craft that rode the rolling swell of the open sea as gracefully as a gull. Pictured above is a late nineteenth-century whaleboat, the product of over a century of experience. The form and light weight of this boat are perfect for easy handling, large carrying capacity, and seaworthiness.

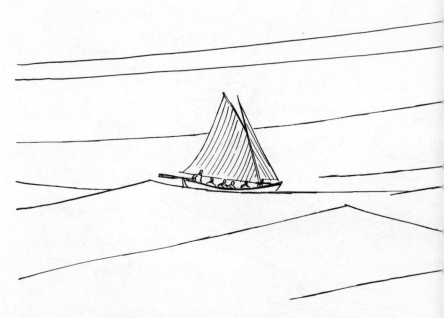

Captain William M. Davis describes a whaleboat in
Nimrod of the Sea, or the American Whaleman, published in
1874:

... The whaleboat is simply as perfect as the combined skill of the
million men who have risked life and limb in service could make
it.... (It) is 28 feet long, sharp and clean cut as a dolphin, bow and
stern swelling amidships to 6 feet, with a bottom round and buoy-
ant. The gunwale amidships, 22 inches above the keel, rises with a
curve to 37 inches at each end, and this rise of bow and stern, with
the clipper-like upper form, gives it a duck-like capacity to top the
oncoming waves, so that it will dryly ride when ordinary boats
would fill. The gunwale and keel, of the best timber, are her heavi-
est parts, and give stiffness to the whole ... Here we have a boat
which two men may lift, and which will make ten miles an hour in
dead chase by the oars alone.

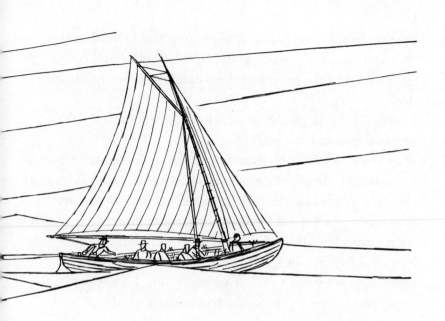

The equipment of the boat consists of a line-tub, in which are coiled 3,000 fathoms (500 feet) of hemp line, with every precaution possible against kinking in the outrun; a mast and sprit-sail; 5 oars; the harpoon and after-oar 14 feet; the tub and bow-oar, 16 feet; and the mid-ship, 18 feet long; so placed that the two shortest and one longest pull against the two 16-feet oars, which arrangement preserves the balance in the encounter when the boat is worked by four oars ... The boat is steered by an oar 22-feet long, which works through a grummet on the stern-post. The gear of the boat consists of 2 live harpoons secured to the side of the boat ... and 2 or 3 lances ... the sharp heads of all these being guarded by well-fitted soft wood sheathes ... The tub-line is secured to the eye of the (harpoon) line ... A hatchet and a sharp knife are placed in the bow-box, convenient for cutting the line, and a water-keg, fire apparatus, candles, lantern, compass, and bandages for wounds, with waif flags on poles, a fluke-spade, and a "drug," or dragging float, complete the equipment of a whale-boat. Among this crowd of dangerous lines and threatening cutting gear, are six pair of legs, belonging to the six skilled boatmen.

Boat spade is a short-handled spade that was carried in the boat and used for cutting a hole in the dead whale. A line was secured in the hole, and the whale towed to the whaleship.

Line tub is the large tub in which the line attached to the harpoon line was carefully coiled.

Waif is a small flag attached to a sharp, pointed staff that was used to indicate a dead whale afloat in the water. It was also used to send signals from a whaleboat to a whaleship.

Boat crotch is a forked wooden device set forward on the right gunwale of the whaleboat. In it were held the "live irons," or first two harpoons to be darted at the whale.

Water keg contained fresh drinking water. This was most important in case the boat was accidentally separated from the whaleship.

Lantern keg is about two feet long and held survival gear: a lantern, candles, flint and steel, matches, tobacco, and hard bread.

Drag, or Drogue, is a block of wood, or as pictured, a canvas or wooden bucket. It was attached to the whale line and flung overboard only on the rare occasions when the line was run out to its end. In the water it acted as a brake and slowed the fleeing whale.

Piggin is a small wooden bucket with one long stave, or ear, that was used to bail water from the boat.

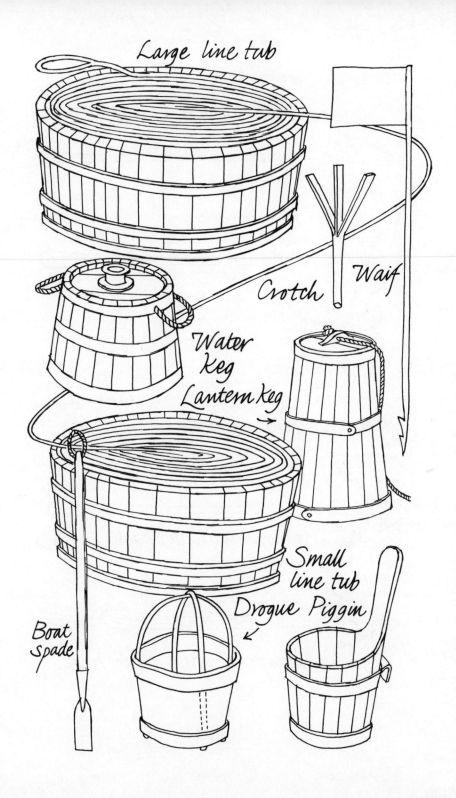

Large line tub

Waif

Crotch

Water Keg

Lantern Keg →

Small line tub

Drogue   Piggin

Boat spade

The Temple, or "toggle iron"

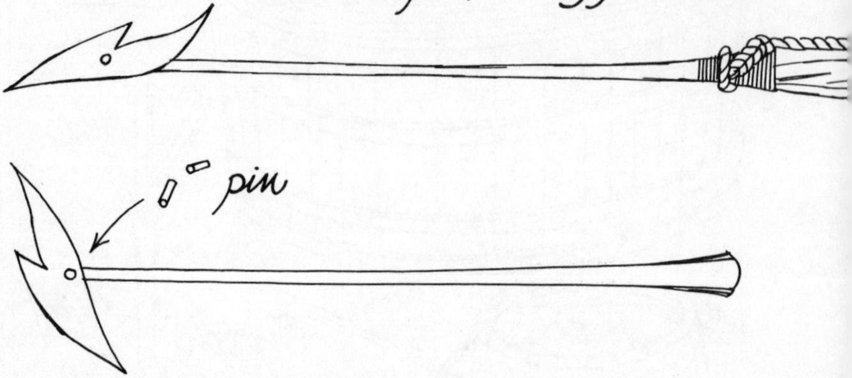

pin

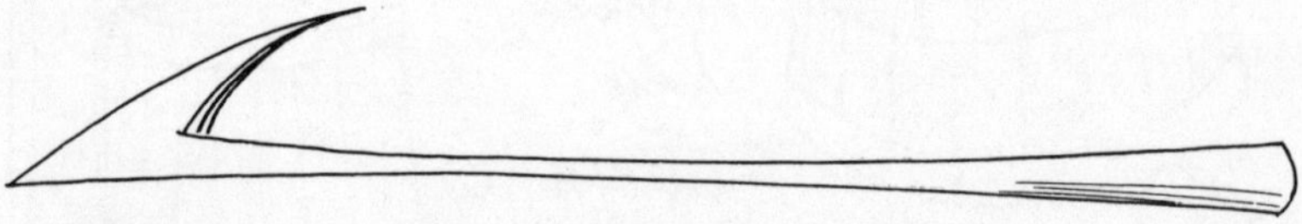

Harpoon with one barb or flue

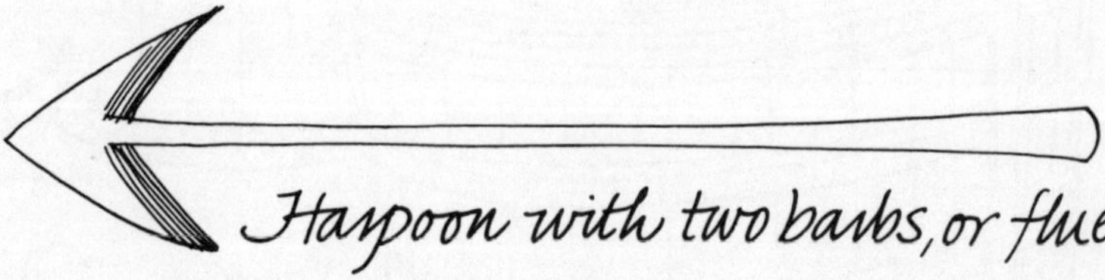

Harpoon with two barbs, or flues

Harpoon with stone head

Whalecraft

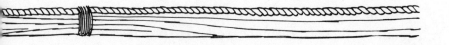

Whalecraft is the name for the iron weapons used in taking whales. They were carried in the whaleboat. The original harpoon, lower left, was probably developed by Indians of the North Atlantic Coast, and used in the off-shore whaling they are said to have practised. The local Indians, who did not work in iron, would have had to make harpoon barbs from stone and animal bones.

The European colonists improved these and whalemen of later years developed the double-barbed arrow-shaped iron and the single-barbed harpoon

The most effective was the Temple or toggle iron, top. It was invented by Lewis Temple, a Negro blacksmith of New Bedford in 1848. A wooden pin held the head to the shank, until it was driven into the whale's flanks. As the whale bolted away, the pin broke, the toggle head turned a right-angle position to the shank and held fast.

The harpoon, or iron, was used to capture the whale; the hand lance to kill the whale. Of razor-sharp steel, the lance has a flat head and a 5- or 6-foot shank attached to a 6-foot pole of rough wood. (The bark was usually left on the shanks of these lances and harpoons to provide a sure, non-slip grip.) It was driven deep into the whale's lungs by the mate, or boatheader, whose other job was to handle the long steering oar at the stern of the whaleboat. The boat-header commanded in the whaleboat. He gave orders to the men in the boat, and was responsible for the perform-ance of their duty. The harpoon was "pitched" by the harpooner, or boat steerer. His other job was to pull the forward oar in the whaleboat.

When the mate, or boatheader, went forward to kill the whale with the lance, the harpooner went aft to handle the long steering oar. This is why he was also called the boat *steerer,* as well as the harpooner. He and the mate, or boat-*header,* changed places in the boat after it was fast to a whale. Imagine how tricky that must have been in a boat full of men and gear, all the while being pulled along the top of the waves by an angry whale with harpoons stuck in him!

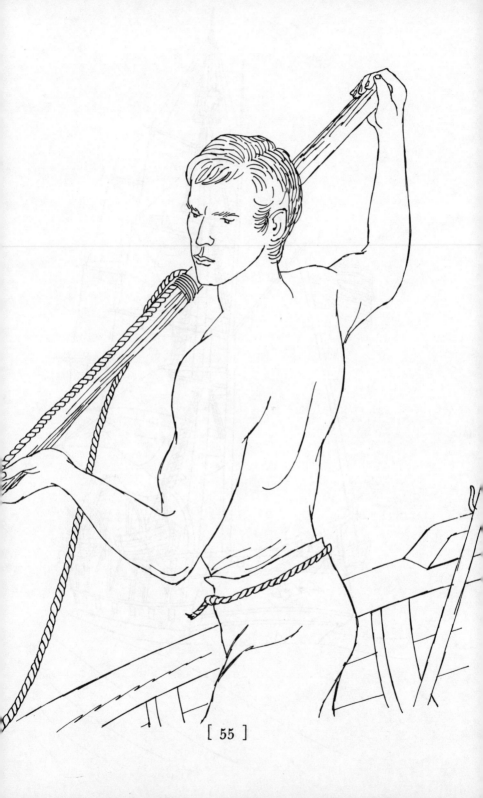

The Lookout

High atop the fore-and-mainmasts of the whaleships were two padded rings or "masthead hoops" where the lookouts were stationed in 2-hour watches, or shifts.

It was the job of these men to search the horizon for the telltale spouts or "blows" of whales. When spouts were seen, the lookout shouted, "A-A-A-A-H BLO-O-O-WS!" or "There she blows," repeated each time the whales spouted.

Imagine that you have just heard the cry of the lookout. You are on a whaleship in the nineteenth century, lazily cruising the ocean in search of whales. At the sound of "BLOWS!" every man aboard the ship springs into action. The whale hunt is on.

"Where away?" the captain shouts.

"Three points off the lee bow. Bl-o-ws, 4 miles off and sperm at that!" If it is a sperm whale, the men can tell. Sperm whales have only one nostril and spout at an angle. All other whales have straight up-and-down spouts.

Then the captain leaps into the rigging to have a look while all hands on board spring into action.

"Flukes! There goes flukes!" shouts the lookout. The whale has gone under. The captain scans the sea with his glasses, and shouts orders to the helmsman at the great steering wheel.

Castoff

The whaleship swings around and heads in the direction of the spouts.

"Stand by to lower the boats!" the captain cries. Then, "Lower away!"

Down the boats go, the lines slipping through the tackle, their crews scampering over the side of the whaleship, leaping lightly and cautiously into the boats. If the climate is warm, the boat crew is barefoot—the scuffing of shoes would be picked up by the highly sensitive hearing of the whale.

The boats head away from the ship in a line with the path of the whale. If the wind is from the right quarter, the mast is stepped in the boat and the sail is raised. But, more often than not, the crew rows to the hunt, each boat racing to be the first "on the whale."

They face the boatheader who steers toward the whale, goading the men at the oars to superhuman effort. The men are forbidden to look back in the direction of the whale, for fear of panicking.

Going-on the Whale

At a command, the harpooner leaves his position at the bow oar, braces himself at the bow of the frail whaleboat and holds the long deadly harpoon in position. The mate, or boatheader, maneuvers the boat to within a few feet of the whale. The harpooner is at the ready, awaiting the order to dart the iron.

"Give it to him!" shouts the mate, and then, "Another! Give him another!" The harpooner's irons sink into the whale.

Perils

"Stern all! Stern all!" shouts the mate. The harpooner tosses out some fathoms of slack line, and changes places with the mate. The crew, pulling desperately at their oars, backs the boat away from the wounded whale and his deadly flukes. These can capsize the fragile boat with a single glancing blow. A wounded, thrashing whale can swamp a boat with little effort.

Line from the harpoon is given a turn around the loggerhead and soaked with sea water to prevent it from burning as it runs out from the line tubs. One of the men picks up some slack line and takes a few more turns on the loggerhead making the boat fast to the whale as it swims away in fury.

The boat skims the water's surface at high speed, pulled along by the mighty power of the whale. This is called a "Nantucket Sleighride." Sleighrides were considered one of the fastest and most thrilling methods of travel then.

Reaching His Life

Sometimes the whale dives deeply, or sounds, and the men have to watch the line, lest the whale break water, or "breech" directly below them. In due time the whale tires. The crew take up the line, until they are close enough to kill the whale. The mate stands in the bow where the harpooner was poised earlier. These men are skilled from years of experience. To sail a boat stealthily up to a whale and to kill him with a lance takes an enormous amount of know-how as well as great personal courage.

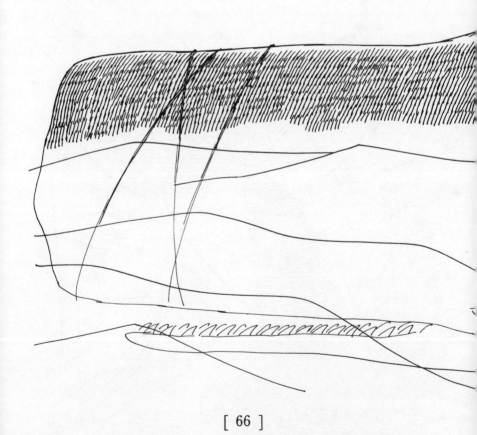

The mate then sinks the razor-sharp lance deep into the lungs of the whale, "churning" it or thrusting it up and down in an exhausting physical effort to hasten death. The whale's breathing slows, blood spouts from its nostrils.

The mate orders the crew to back off, get clear of the dying monster. As the whale thrashes in circles, the sea is churned to a bloody foam. In a last terrifying convulsion, the great whale ends its struggle. It rolls over on its side, its head toward the sun, its dorsal fin clear of the water.

The men in the whaleboat rejoice, having cheated death themselves. In their jargon the whale is now "fin out."

Cutting-in

Once the whale is dead, the mate cuts a hole in its head. To this he attaches a line. The crew then tows the whale back to the whaleship.

If there were more whales to be attacked in the area, then a waif, or identifying flag, would be stuck into the floating body of the dead whale until the boats could return to claim their prizes.

The whale is held alongside the ship by a fluke chain passed around its tail, and pulled tight by a windlass. The ship shortens sail but makes headway, keeping the whale in tow. A cutting-in stage is swung out directly above the carcass. The experienced mates use long, sharp cutting spades and balance on a swaying platform—steadied only by the waist-high iron railing. They have to work quickly if sharks are feeding on the whale—otherwise great chunks of flesh and blubber that could be processed into valuable oil would be devoured.

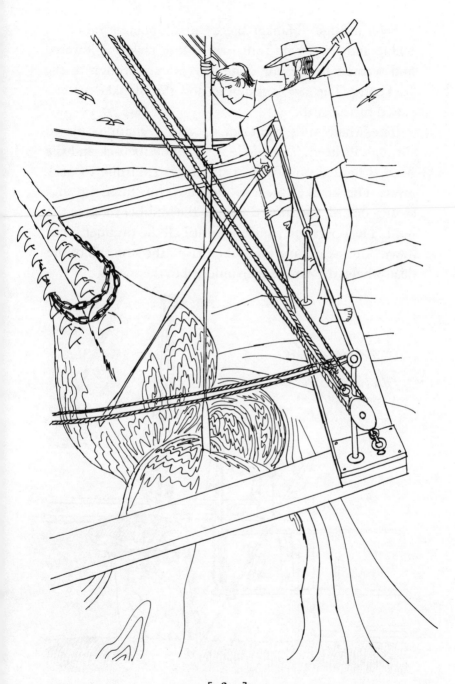

Soon a huge "blanket piece" of blubber is raised by tackle and the whale rolls over. More tackle is lowered and secured to the jaw. The officers cut through to the backbone. The jaw is removed and the blanket piece is raised further still.

The whale rolls right-side-up and a chain is passed through its head. The whale is rolled on its back and the head is hauled on board as the mates continue to hack away. The blanket piece is then hove up high, cut and swung aboard, and stowed away in the blubber room in the hold. The operation continues until all the blubber is cut away. After searching for ambergris in the stomach of the dead whale, the carcass is abandoned to the sharks.

Hoisting the blanket piece

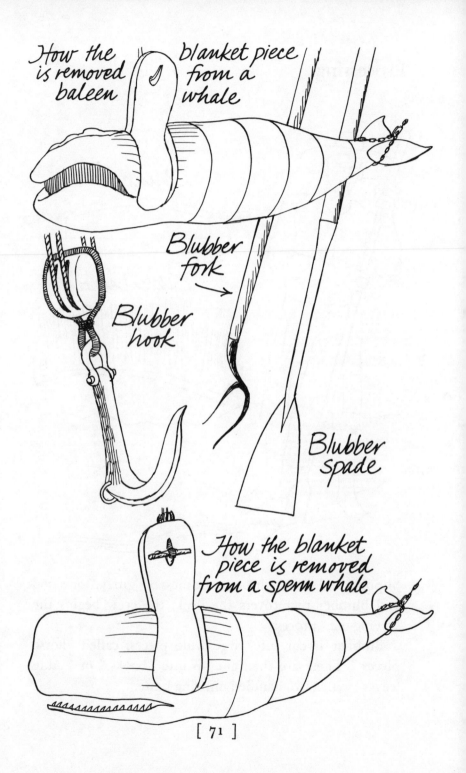

How the is removed baleen

blanket piece from a whale

Blubber fork →

Blubber hook

Blubber spade

How the blanket piece is removed from a sperm whale

[71]

Processing

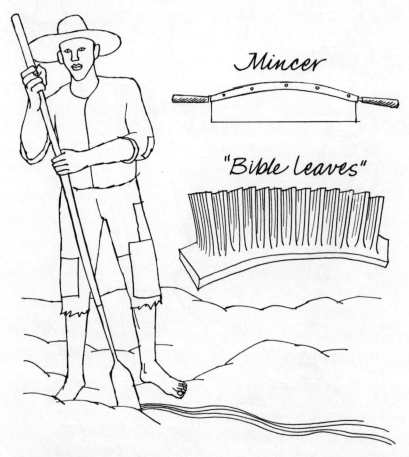

Mincer

"Bible Leaves"

Slipping and sliding through the mess of "gurry," or blood and blubber that covers the deck, the crew begins the "trying-out" process.

Blubber is cut into large wide pieces, called "horse pieces." These are then cut up into "books," or "bible leaves" with a two-handled mincing knife.

Try works

Try pot

They are put into the try-pots and boiled or "tried out." The oil is bailed out into a large copper cooling tank set next to the brick tryworks. The scraps remaining in the pots are skimmed off and used to feed the fires.

Once the oil is cool, it is bailed into casks which are secured to the bulwarks.

The tryworks, a distinctive feature of all whaling ships, consists of two, or occasionally three, large iron try-pots of about 250 gallon capacity, set in a brick furnace on the main deck. The wooden deck is insulated from the intense

Bailer

Skimmer

[73]

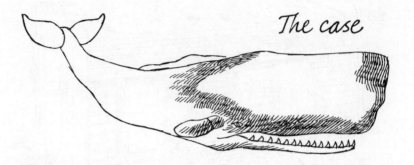

heat of the fires by a foot-high trough kept filled with sea water. This is called a "goose pen." The first course of bricks is set in it. The masonry walls of the bricked-in try-works are attached to the deck by huge angle irons, or "knees." Sliding iron fire doors enclose the roaring fire and protect the men working at the try-pots.

If the men are cutting-in a sperm whale, they "bail the case" for spermaceti oil. The "case" of the sperm whale is in the upper half of the head and contains an enormous amount of pure spermaceti oil that makes up the major portion of the sperm whale's head. The case is opened and the clear white liquid bailed out. Often, the men stand up to their waists in this oozy material. They don't mind because it is supposed to be good for the skin and is used to make skin creams. The spermaceti oil hardens somewhat and becomes waxy after being in the air, so it is then carefully heated and funneled into barrels.

The "junk" or lower half of the forehead above the skull contains oil and spermaceti so it is cut up in horse pieces and tried out. The flesh of the sperm whale's head contains no blood vessels and is pure white. It is called "white horse" by the whalemen. Parts of the head not used are thrown over the side.

Bailing the case

Dipper

Case bucket

Cask

[75]

Seamen and Scrimshaw

In the beginning, the crew of a whaling ship was almost entirely made up of local men and boys. These boys of coastal New England got their sea legs at an early age and advanced rapidly in rank, becoming first mates in their teens, captains and masters of their own vessels in their early twenties.

Their places in the ranks, or crews, were filled by "greenies," or "green horns," young farmers from the hills. Later, in the 1830's and '40's, these landsmen found jobs in the new factories springing up in New England. There they could earn twice as much and stay dry and alive, too.

The clipper ship became famous about mid-century and captured the fancy of young men who might otherwise have gone to sea in the whale fishery. With the clipper came higher wages for seamen, and much shorter cruises. Now it was hard to find men willing to spend four or five years on one voyage.

The crews became a mixture of Anglo-Saxons, Azorean Portuguese, Cape Verdean Portuguese with a sprinkling of French-Canadians, Germans, Scandinavians, American Negroes, and Polynesians from Fiji, Samoa, and Hawaii (all lumped together in one group as "Kanakas," natives of the Hawaiian Islands).

The crews lived in crowded, filthy quarters infested with bugs and rats and ventilated by one small hatch which had to be closed in stormy weather. The ceiling or "overhead" was so low that a man of more than average height could not straighten up. Two tiers of bunks took up most of the available space. A row of sea chests left only a small patch of deck remaining. It was here that the men ate and gambled at cards when they were off duty.

The whaling seaman spent very little of his time in pursuit of whales. The vessels, their bottoms often encrusted with barnacles and tons of marine growth, moved slowly. It took them months to get to and from the whaling grounds. And there was never any guarantee that whales would be found. There were two and three times as many men crowded into whaling ships as the clipper ships twice their size. Discipline was not as severe; the men stood fewer watches and had more leisure time. Often, as their log books or journals testify, they were bored beyond belief.

To help pass the hours, they took to carving and engraving the teeth and jawbone of the sperm whale into a primitive form of folk art called "scrimshaw." The roughly textured teeth were carefully filed and rubbed smooth. Then, original designs or those copied from newspapers or magazines were engraved on the polished surface with a sharp tool, such as a sailmaker's needle. Paint, tar, or soot was rubbed into the scratched lines to bring out the design in detail.

Carved scrimshaw took the form of jagging wheels, as these pie crust crimpers were called, letter openers, small sculptural pieces, swifts (a collapsible reel for winding yarn), ship models, forks and spoons, napkin rings, decorative combs, and cane heads.

Authentic scrimshaw is much sought after by today's collectors; even newly made pieces find a ready market in gift shops. Most whaling museums have many examples on display in their collections.

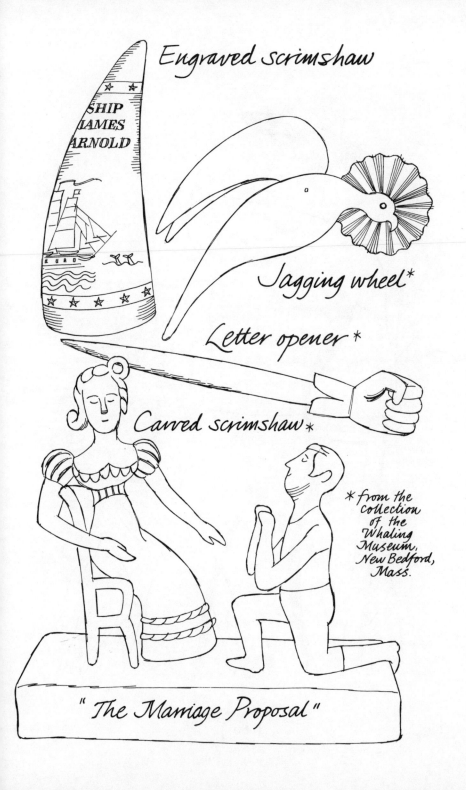

Engraved scrimshaw

SHIP JAMES ARNOLD

Jagging wheel*

Letter opener*

Carved scrimshaw*

*from the collection of the Whaling Museum, New Bedford, Mass.

"The Marriage Proposal"

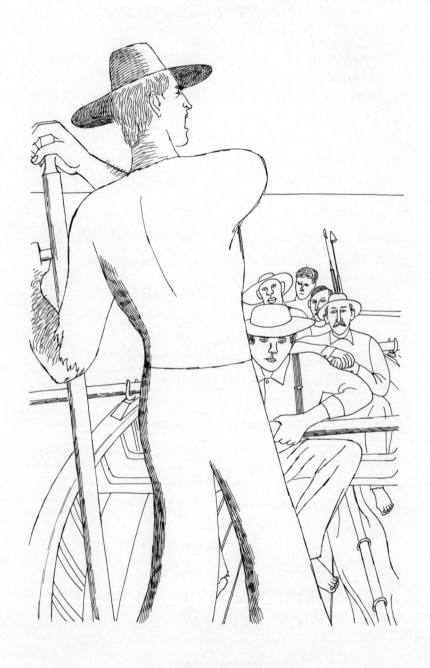

Boatheaders and Boat Steerers

In contrast to the wretched living conditions of the fo'c's'le, the quarters of the ship's specialists and officers were tolerable, and the captain lived in comparative comfort.

The officers: first mate (usually referred to as "the mate"), second mate, third and others, served as boatheaders (see pages 54-66). They handled the long steering oar until it was time to move forward and kill the whale with the hand lance.

The harpooner, with whom they changed places, was also the boat steerer (who pulled the forward oar). He was not an officer but held a rating on a par with the ship's carpenter and cooper, ship smith and cook. Together, these specialists bunked in small staterooms just aft of amidships.

The officers, in larger rooms further aft, shared the quarterdeck with the captain. The pay was good, the food a bit better than that served the crew.

All that was required to make the grade were goodly amounts of skill and daring, and a certain ability for making others work. This often called for less than heroic qualities; some ship's officers were vicious bullies and the harsh treatment of men under their command is appalling. Sometimes they were, in turn, driven mercilessly by cruel, overbearing captains.

The Master

The Captain was called the "master" of the vessel and he was truly that—master of all he surveyed. Once upon the high seas he was responsible only to the owners of the vessel. He had the authority to punish the men, sell the cargo and even the ship itself, if need be. He handed out justice to the crew (whippings and the lockup in irons were common punishment for troublemakers). He served as ship's doctor, practising hit-or-miss medicine from a box of assorted drugs. His quarters were comfortable, often shared with his wife and children who came along for the voyage.

Whenever a whaleship "spoke," hailed another at sea, the captain and his wife went over for a "gam," or friendly meeting. If time permitted, the crews and officers "gammed" also. The captain's wife would be carried in a "gamming" chair fastened to tackle in the manner of a bosun's chair and lowered to a whaleboat. Sometimes a gamming chair would be an ordinary shipboard "captain's chair" attached by ropes to the tackle. Others, as the one shown here, were more enclosed, and much preferred by the ladies.

Almost all masters of whaleships had worked their way up from the fo'c's'le and had a great deal of practical ability as ship handlers.

There were of course, kind and generous masters, concerned for the comfort and well-being of the men who served under them. Sometimes this was disastrous with the wrong crew. Some barbarous mutinies took place on vessels commanded by decent, considerate masters.

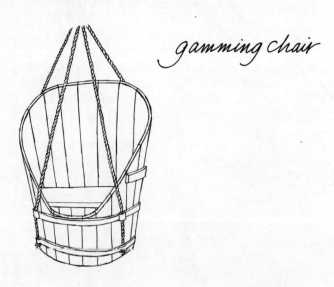

gamming chair

The quarterdeck of a whaling schooner

Master

Helmsman

Big Business

Whaling was big business—a huge enterprise that brought millions of dollars to the towns of Nantucket, Edgartown, Provincetown, Fairhaven, Dartmouth, and New Bedford in Massachusetts; Bristol in Rhode Island; New London, Mystic, and Stonington in Connecticut; and Sag Harbor, Long Island.

But it was New Bedford which prospered the most. Here great fortunes were made as the price of whale oil rose. Then petroleum was discovered in 1859. It soon was selling for one-fifth the price of whale oil and the end of whaling drew near.

In whaling's heyday, profits from a voyage were occasionally stupendous, some vessels averaging almost 100 per cent profit on each voyage. Merchants and shipowners put up money to fit out a whaling expedition and sold the oil when and if the ship came back with a cargo. Out of the profits from the sale of the oil and whalebone, the owners would pay "lays," or shares to the officers and crew. The officers, of course, earned more.

Out of the seaman's pay would come charges from the "slop chest," or ship's store of clothing, tobacco, and other articles to be sold to the seaman on the voyage. The slop chest added to the profits of the owners, and often the captain shared a big percentage of it too. Also taken from a man's pay were charges for fitting out and clearing the ship from port, a share of the medicine chest, interest on money loaned the owners, and so on. The poor foremast hand went ashore more often than not with less than $200 for a four-year voyage! The captain usually did very well. The owners took a large share, almost always more than half. Is it any wonder that so many beautiful mansions are found in all the old whaling cities?

A whaling ship "hove down" for repairs

Ship Fitting

Whaleships were built all along the New England coast in shipyards that have long since disappeared. They were not big vessels but they were extremely well put together. They could withstand heavy seas, storms and voyages of long duration.

The first whaleships went to sea with uncoppered bottoms and were prey to all sorts of marine growth and shipworms that are plentiful in the warm oceans of the world. It became the custom to overhaul the ships at various Pacific Islands, "heaving them down" whenever possible to repair the damages to the hull. A familiar sight along the wharves in New Bedford, too, must have been that of the "hovedown" whaleships having their hulls caulked and recoppered.

[88]

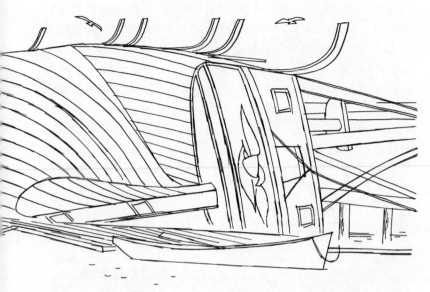

Before a ship left for a voyage, it was important to see that she was seaworthy. Her fastenings, timbers, and planking were examined carefully for decay. Caulkers made her seams tight by driving oakum into them. The hull was then covered with sheets of copper or Taunton metal, a special yellow metal that would protect the bottom from barnacles and the boring teredo worms.

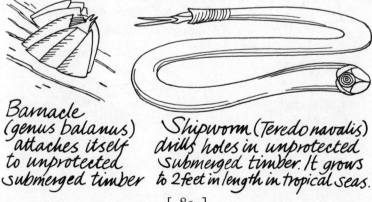

Barnacle (genus *balanus*) attaches itself to unprotected submerged timber

Shipworm (*Teredo navalis*) drills holes in unprotected submerged timber. It grows to 2 feet in length in tropical seas.

All movable parts and equipment were taken off a ship being refitted, examined and repaired. (If the next cruise were to be in Arctic waters, the bow would be reinforced to protect against possible damage by huge blocks of floating ice.) Spars and rigging would be overhauled, canvas replaced and repaired, whaling gear put in order, new equipment forged, and new casks would be coopered. The following pages will touch briefly on these essential trades and occupations.

A caulker at work

Often, the caulker could sit at his work on what might be called a "caulker's rocker."

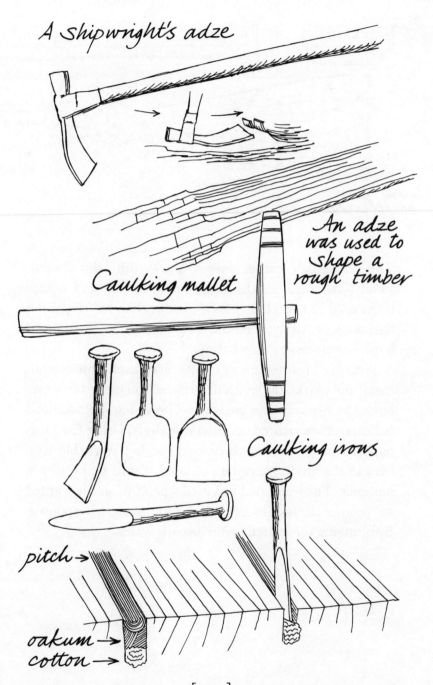

A shipwright's adze

An adze was used to shape a rough timber

Caulking mallet

Caulking irons

pitch →

oakum →
cotton →

Blacksmith

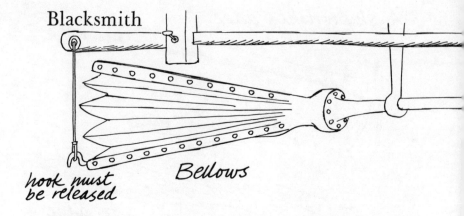

hook must
be released

Bellows

The whalecraft maker was a blacksmith who forged, welded and repaired the many metal fittings and equipment used in the whale fishery. In his shop he forged the harpoons or "irons," lances, blubber spades, hooks and hardware necessary in whaling.

Wearing a leather apron to protect himself from the hot metal and sparks, the smith heated the iron in the large firebox. The fire was kept roaring by pumping the overhead bellows which created considerable draft. Using the long-handled tongs, the smith carried the hot workable iron over to the anvil where he pounded it into shape with a hammer. The water pen was used when the smith wanted to "temper" or harden a piece of iron, such as a harpoon—by plunging the heated metal into the water.

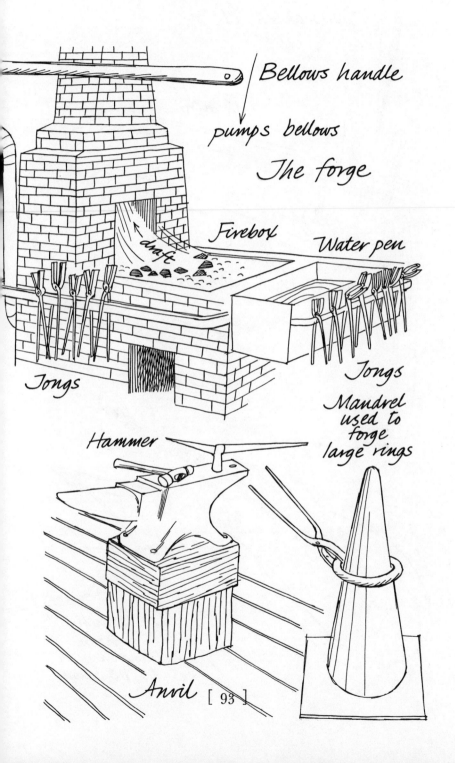

Bellows handle

pumps bellows

The forge

Firebox

Water pen

draft

Jongs

Jongs

Mandrel
used to
forge
large rings

Hammer

Anvil [93]

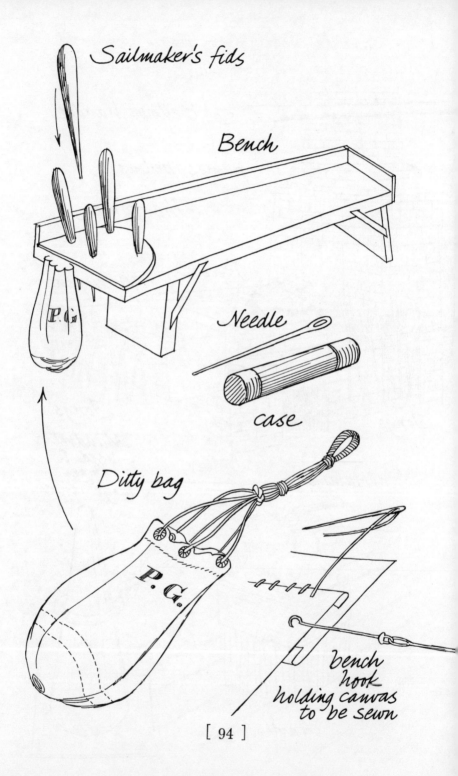

Sailmaker's fids

Bench

Needle

case

Ditty bag

P.G

P.G.

bench
hook
holding canvas
to be sewn

Sailmaking

The sail loft was where new canvas was made into sails and old canvas repaired. The canvas-covered sailmaker's bench was a very low crude affair. At one end hung the canvas ditty bag which held the sailmaker's gear. This included large sailmaker's needles and a leather palm, bench hook, sail twine, serving mallet, marlinespikes, and fids.

The needles were pushed through the heavy canvas by hand, the eye of the needle seated securely in the iron fitting of the palm. The canvas was held flat by the bench hook. Marlinespikes and fids were used in splicing, the prickers for small work.

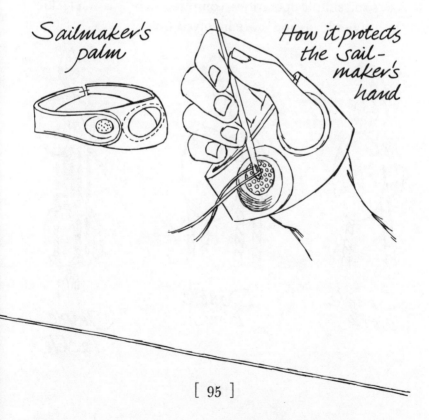

Sailmaker's palm

How it protects the sail-maker's hand

Rigging

The rigging of a ship consists of all the ropes and chains needed to support the masts and move the yards, booms, gaffs, and canvas.

The rigger's bench held the rope for splicing; the fids separated the strands. The bosun's chairs were used to carry the riggers aloft where they often worked—high above the ship's deck. The rigging had to be especially well done so that the ship would sail properly and stand up to the force of gales and wild storms. Tackle, shown below, was the equipment used for raising or lowering various heavy shipboard gear. It consisted of a rope and pulleys or blocks. Small simple tackle was used for light loads and simple operations, complicated blocks and tackle for heavier loads and more involved work.

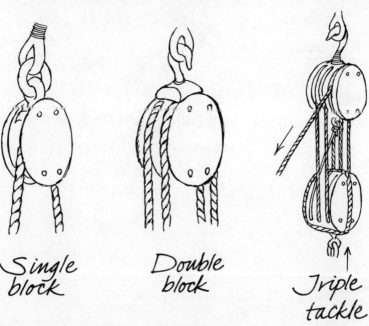

Single block

Double block

Triple tackle

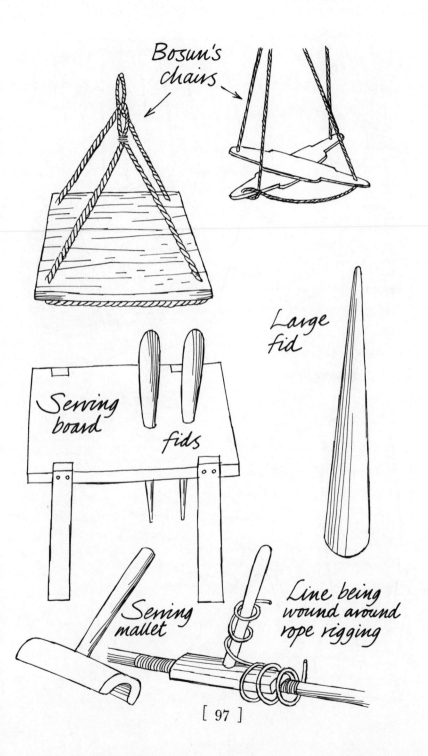

Bosun's chairs

Large fid

Serving board

fids

Serving mallet

Line being wound around rope rigging

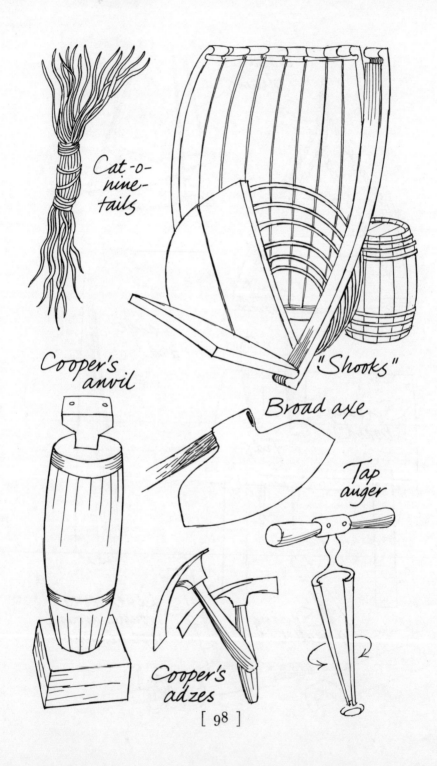

Cat-o-nine-tails

"Shooks"

Cooper's anvil

Broad axe

Tap auger

Cooper's adzes

[98]

Cooperage

The cooper made casks by hand from white oak, split with the grain. Rushes filled the seams as caulking. Some of these huge casks measured 4 feet in diameter across the top or "head" and stood 5 feet high. When full such a cask held about a ton of oil. They were designed so that they could be knocked down and stowed aboard ship in bundles, or "shooks," as they were called, and assembled when needed on the voyage.

The cooper's anvil was used to repair bent and damaged hoops; tap augers were used for cutting tapered holes in the barrel (where it was filled); the adzes were used in shaping the barrel staves; the mallet for driving hoops on the barrels. The long heavy cooper's joiner plane is curious. Unlike other planes which are drawn over wood, this one remained stationary and the staves were drawn over it.

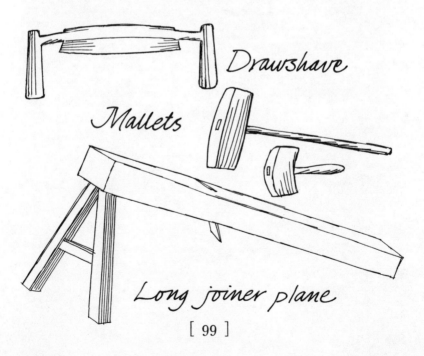

Drawshave

Mallets

Long joiner plane

Whaling Through the Years

Shore whaling was the method used by the early settlers. They would mount lookouts along the beach and wait for stranded whales and blackfish.

In 1690 Ichabod Paddock of Cape Cod was invited to Nantucket to teach the art of whaling to the people there.

In 1712 Christopher Hussey of Nantucket was blown out to sea in a storm and while out on the briny deep he took two sperm whales. Then the hunting of whales began in earnest. The tryworks were moved from shore onto the decks of the whaling vessels which now put out to sea for weeks at a time.

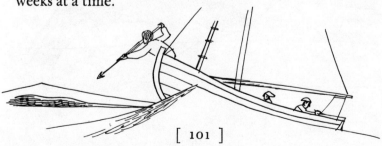

The Revolutionary War and the War of 1812 brought misery and hardship and near ruin to New England whaling. Whalemen were made prisoners by the British and some forced to work on British vessels. Others fled to Canada, England and France.

Whaling recovered after the War of 1812 and was in its golden age until the Civil War. New grounds were located in the uncharted frozen wastes of the Arctic. There the Arctic bowhead whale, heavy with oil, was found. In 1857 New Bedford had 329 whaleships in her fleet.

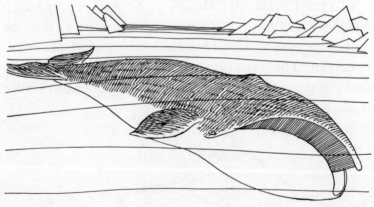

In 1865 the Confederate raider *Shenandoah* burned twenty-five whaleships caught helpless in the Arctic. At least fifty whaleships were lost in the Civil War, most of them large ships, important to the industry.

Six years later, in 1871, thirty-three more were crushed by Arctic ice. The captains, forewarned by early snow in August, paid no heed to the warnings of the Eskimos that an early winter was at hand. By September all vessels had to be abandoned, though over 1,200 whalemen and wives and children miraculously escaped unharmed.

In 1876, twelve more vessels were lost to the ice, in 1879 two more, in 1888 a heavy gale took five more ships with all hands lost; in 1897 and 1898 other vessels were imprisoned in the ice and left abandoned.

In 1859 petroleum was discovered in Pennsylvania. Soon kerosene—made from petroleum—replaced whale oil as a fuel for lamps. The low cost of it destroyed the whale oil market for all time.

John R. Manta, last New Bedford whaler

By 1920 only two large whaleships were operating out of New England ports. They were the bark *Wanderer,* wrecked off Cuttyhunk in 1924, and the *Charles W. Morgan,* now a shipboard museum in Old Mystic, Connecticut. The last whaling voyage out of New Bedford was made by the schooner *John R. Manta,* in 1927.

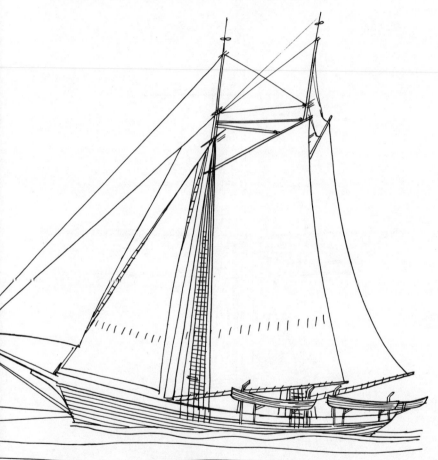

Charles W. Morgan, at Mystic Seaport, Connecticut

GLOSSARY

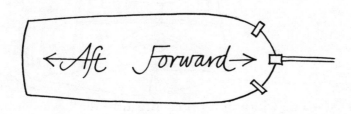

AFT—Near or towards the stern, or rear end of the vessel.

AMBERGRIS—A dark brown, waxy substance found in the intestines of sperm whales—used in the making of perfumes.

AZOREANS—Natives of the Azores Islands (Portuguese), about 1,500 miles west of Portugal in the Atlantic Ocean.

BAIL—To dip water or liquid from one thing to another; to bail (dip) oil from one cask to another; to bail (remove) water from the bottom of the boat.

BALEEN—The plates or blades of black "whalebone" found in the mouths of whales without teeth. Baleen is made of the same material, "keratin," as fingernails, cows' horns, and hair.

BARNACLES—A form of shellfish that attaches itself to rocks, timbers, and the bottoms of ships.

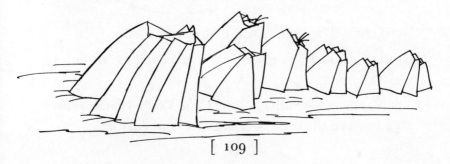

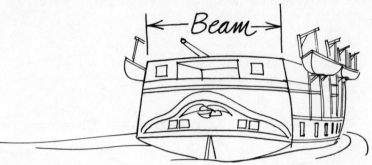

BEAM—The width of a vessel. Broad in the beam means very wide.

BLOW—Spout. The breath of the whale is seen as spray—spouted, or blown from the whale's nostril or blowhole on the top of his head.

BLUBBER—The thick oily outer blanket of fat that protects the whale from cold and the pressure of ocean depths. Oil is obtained from "trying," or cooking the blubber.

BOOM—A spar, or pole used to extend the bottom of a sail.

BOW—Rhymes with cow. The forward part of the vessel.

BRIT—The food of baleen whales. Small, shrimplike creatures, also called krill.

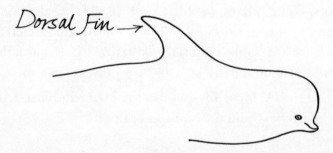

CACHALOT—The French name for sperm whale.

CANVAS—Another name for sails, which were made of canvas.

CAPE VERDEANS—Natives of the Cape Verde Islands (Portuguese), off the coast of Senegal in West Africa.

CAPSIZE—To upset or overturn a vessel.

CASE—The upper half of the sperm whale's forehead outside the skull.

CASK—A barrel-shaped container. Casks were of various sizes, some of them very large.

CAULK—To fill up openings, to make seams and joints watertight.

DORSAL FIN—The fin on the back of a fish or whale. It is sometimes seen out of water while the creature is swimming near the surface, as with sharks, killer whales, and porpoises.

FATHOM—6 feet. Fathoms are used in measuring rope, and in measuring the depths of the sea. The rope is said to be so many fathoms long, and the oceans so many fathoms deep.

FIJI ISLANDERS—Natives of the Fiji Islands of the South Pacific, east of Australia and north of New Zealand.

FIT OUT—Getting a vessel ready for sailing.

FLIPPERS—The broad, flat limbs that whales and other mammals such as dolphins and seals have.

FLUKE—The lobes, or horizontal part of the whale's tail.

FURROW—The lined grooves in the whale's throat, or undersides.

Fo'c's'le—The forecastle of a vessel, the upper deck forward of the mainmast or the space below it, where the crew had its quarters.

Gaff—This is the top spar on which the upper edge of a fore-and-aft sail is rigged. See drawing.

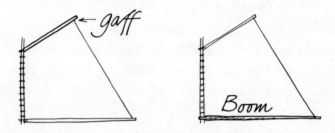

Gear—A word used for many things, from equipment to personal belongings.

Gimbal—A fixture that keeps an article level, no matter how much the support of it tips or moves about.

Grummet, or Grommet—An eyelet, ring, or hole with a reinforced edge.

Gunwale—Pronounced "gunnel"—the upper edge of a vessel's or boat's side.

Hatch—An opening in the deck of a vessel.

Helmsman—The man at the steering wheel of a vessel. Also, the man at the tiller of a boat or smaller craft.

Hove—Heaved, hoisted.

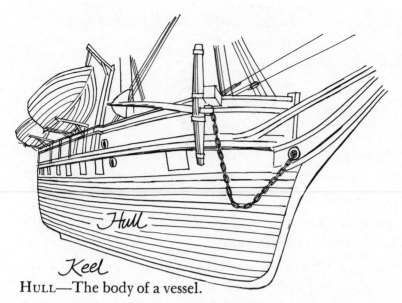

Hull

Keel

HULL—The body of a vessel.

JUMPING SHIP—A common expression used by sailors that means to desert, or run away when their vessel is in port.

JUNK—The lower half of the sperm whale's forehead, above the skull.

KANAKA—A native of the Hawaiian Islands. The name sometimes given to all Polynesian sailors serving aboard whaleships.

KEEL—A heavy timber running lengthwise at the bottom of a vessel.

KRILL—See Brit.

LANDSMAN—A sailor who is on his first sea voyage. One who has never been to sea before.

LIBERTY—Shore leave for sailors; time off-duty ashore.

LOB-TAILING—The term whalemen used to describe a whale in the act of pounding the surface of the water with his flukes.

Loggerhead

LOGGERHEAD—The stubby post in the stern of the whale-boat around which the whale line is snubbed, or checked, as it is run out.

MELON—The upper half of the forehead, or case, of the pilot whale, or blackfish.

MUTINY—When the crew of a vessel riots and tries to take it over by force.

OAKUM—A loose material made from picking apart old hemp ropes. It is used for caulking seams.

PACK ICE—Flocks or groups of icebergs.

PILOT—A person licensed to take vessels in and out of port. A vessel usually takes a pilot aboard when it enters a harbor or dangerous waters.

QUARTERDECK—The upper deck abaft, or to the rear of the mainmast. The part of the vessel below which the officers had their quarters. See drawing.

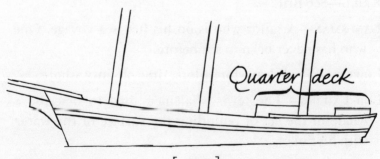

Quarter deck

RAIDER—During the Civil War, the Confederate States Navy had a number of vessels designed to attack Federal shipping. These were called raiders. They would strike quickly and destroy whatever they could. Common practice was to allow the whaling crews to leave the whaleship in whaleboats, and then burn the ship to the waterline.

RATING—The rank of men serving aboard ship. The captain had the highest rank, the first mate the next, and so on.

RIGGING—The ropes and chains used to stay the masts, and support the spars, and control the sails of a vessel.

SAMOANS—Natives of the Samoan Islands in the South Pacific, east of the Fiji Islands.

SCOOPS—What the whalemen called the great gulps of water taken by baleen whales when feeding.

SHIPPING A CREW—Enlisting men aboard, signing them on for a voyage.

SHORTEN SAIL—To take in sail so that less canvas is exposed to the wind. To slow down the vessel.

SPAR—The name for any round timber such as a mast, boom, gaff, or yard, used aboard ship.

Sprit sail on a whaleboat

SPRIT SAIL—A sail extended by a sprit or spar which crosses a fore-and-aft sail diagonally. Such sails were sometimes used in whaleboats.

STEERAGE—The quarters of the harpooners and ship's specialists. This was just abaft of the mainmast and forward of the ship's cabin, or officers' quarters. Steerage is the term also used for the part of a vessel just under the cabin in passenger liners of that day. Here were the bunks and quarters of those who paid the lowest fares.

STEPPED—The mast of a vessel is stepped when it is put in place, the bottom of it secured well below deck.

STOW—To put things away in their proper place. In shipboard terms "gear," equipment, is "stowed away."

TACKLE—The rigging and gear of a ship used with blocks and pulleys and other work gear.

TRY—To melt, or separate. The whale oil was "tryed out" from the blubber in "try-pots." The "try-pots" were set in the "tryworks."

WATCH—A watch was a period of time, usually of four hours, in which a man was on deck, ready for duty. Watch also had another meaning. The watch was the whole group of men who were on deck, ready for duty, at the time. Usually it was one half of all the officers and men aboard ship.

WHALECRAFT—The iron weapons used in whaling such as harpoons, lances, and blubber spades.

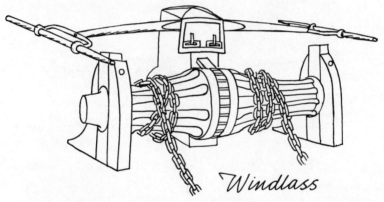

Windlass

WINDLASS—A machine for raising heavy gear, such as an anchor chain. It consists of a drum or cylinder that is turned by crank or lever. The chain or rope is wound up on the drum of the windlass.

YARD—A long, round, tapering timber that supports and extends a square sail.

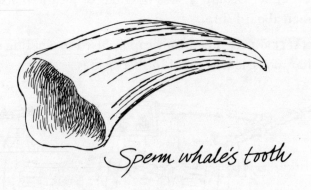

Sperm whale's tooth

BOOKS ABOUT WHALING

Helpful books about the subject of whaling:

ASH, CHRISTOPHER, *Whaler's Eye*, Macmillan, New York, 1962.

CHURCH, ALBERT COOK, *Whale Ships and Whaling*, Norton, New York, 1960.

COOK, J. J. AND WISNER, W. L., *Warrior Whale*, Dodd, Mead, New York, 1966.

HEGARTY, REGINALD B., *The Rope's End*, Houghton Mifflin, Boston, 1965.

HOUGH, HENRY BEETLE, *Great Days of Whaling*, Houghton Mifflin, Boston, 1958.

HUNTINGTON, GALE, *Songs the Whalemen Sang*, Barre Publishers, Barre, Mass., 1964.

JOHNSTON, JOHANNA, *Whale's Way*, Doubleday, New York, 1965.

MELVILLE, HERMAN, *Moby Dick*, New American Library, New York, 1962.

RIEDMAN, S. R. AND GUSTAFSON, E. T., *Home is the Sea: for Whales*, Rand McNally, Chicago, 1966.

SANDERSON, IVAN T., *Follow the Whale*, Little, Brown, Boston, 1956.

SHAPIRO, IRWIN, *Story of Yankee Whaling*, American Heritage, New York, 1959.

STACKPOLE, EDOUARD A., *Sea Hunters*, Lippincott, Philadelphia, 1953.

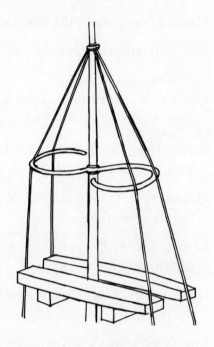

Masthead hoops

INDEX

ABOUT THE AUTHOR

Paul Giambarba's graphic designs have won awards and recognition in the United States and abroad. From 1955 to 1960 he worked and traveled extensively in Europe, settling on Cape Cod upon his return home, where he now lives with his wife and two children. He has been a weekly contributor to Scholastic Magazines periodicals for elementary school children for over ten years. In 1965, he began The Scrimshaw Press in an effort to make abundantly illustrated original material available in paperback form at modest prices.

Books by Paul Giambarba

WHALES, WHALING AND WHALECRAFT

SURFMEN AND LIFESAVERS

EARLY EXPLORERS OF AMERICA

CAPE COD SEASHORE LIFE

AROUND CAPE COD WITH CAP'N GOODY

GOING WHALING WITH CAP'N GOODY